Peaceful Pieces

Poems and Quilts About Peace

Anna Grossnickle Hines

Henry Holt and Company • New York

Making an Entrance

Will peace come with drums?
Be heralded by trumpets?
Prance in waving red
and gold banners?
Will peace make
a great noisy show?

Or will it slip in quietly,
the voice of one lone flute
floating almost unnoticed,
blue, melodic, calm
until, surprised, we say
Ahh . . . this is peace.

An Invitation

O Peace,
why are you such
an infrequent guest?
So timid,
. . . elusive?
See? There is room.
I've banished anger
to the cellar,
pushed fear into the attic,
kept selfishness busy
on the back porch,
and prayed
for you to come.
So why is it, Peace,
that you won't stay?

Where I Live

Where I live the breeze
blows gently across the pond,
the sky is clear and blue,
trees grow tall,
and the song of birds floats in the air.
Where I live people talk instead of fight,
listen instead of talk,
respect and honor differences.
Where I live the hungry are fed,
the sick healed,
the lost returned
safe to their homes.
Where I live there is laughter
and song
and dance.
Where I live there is a stillness,
an openness,
a space for ideas to be born.
Where I live there is no need of fear.
Where there is no fear I live.
Where I live is as big as your heart
and as small as the universe.
I am peace.
Will you have me live with you?

Sure Cure

My sister and I were fighting.
We couldn't get along.
She said I moved her game piece.
I said she was wrong.
She said I was stupid.
I said she was worse
and made a nasty face at her.
She let out a curse.

Mom said, "Stop this bickering
before it comes to blows."
She made us stand together
touching nose to nose.
"How long?" we asked; she answered,
"We'll just see how it goes."

We stood there looking cross-eyed
at our noses touching tips
and feeling rather silly
while pinching up our lips
to try to stop the giggles—
mine started in my toes.
It's hard to keep on fighting
when you're touching nose to nose.

Peace: A Recipe

Open minds—at least two.
Willing hearts—the same.
Rinse well with compassion.
Stir in a fair amount of trust.
Season with forgiveness.
Simmer in a sauce of respect.
A dash of humor brightens the flavor.

Best served with hope.

Forgiveness

COMPASSION

RESPECT

What Would You Choose?

The other kids say
don't play with Sheila
she's got cooties
but when I see her
on the playground
alone
I think
what if that was me?
And choose to share
my jump rope.

Pulling nits from my hair
my mother says
maybe you should have
listened to those kids
but even as I flinch
from the tugs
of the fine-toothed comb
I know
I will play with Sheila
again.

Weightless

Dark and heavy,
anger presses
my pinched heart
into my stomach.
But . . .
when I forgive,
when I truly forgive,
my feather heart
lifts
floats
light
free
spacious enough
to take in
the whole
wonderful
world.

On the River

P addles
E tch ripples as
A wakening birdsong
C reates serene
E choes

Links

Two pebbles plink.
Intersecting circles cover
the whole pond.

The Stream

We pause,
my friend and I,
on a small bridge.
Above and beyond us
water tumbles
over stones,
splashes freely into pools,
while beneath us, it stands
still as a photograph,
twigs and leaves
suspended on
the glassy surface.

How can this be?
Curiosity draws me streamside.
"Be careful," my friend says,
but I have to know
if that one stick caught
broadside between the rocks,
can freeze the surface,
screen the current underneath.
I stretch beyond my reach—
but—Yes! Freed
leaves and twigs rush
downstream!

As we walk on,
I don't even mind
that one foot sloshes.

Calming the Busy Brain

agitated
yapping ideas
chaotic confusing
tumultuous turbulent
frenzied frenetic
hysterical . . .

STOP

let me
relax
take a
deep breath
and
another
one more

now
ideas
I'll take you
one
at a time

Weapons

I have never fired a gun
but have shouted words
that pierced and stung.

I have hurled cutting remarks,
ignited flames with hateful sparks.
I've shot daggers from my eyes
at those I momentarily despised.

I have never fired a gun
but want to learn
to hold my tongue.

When anger flares
it takes just ninety seconds
for the bio-chemical explosion
in your brain
to be all through.
Finished. Flushed
completely from your cells.
One minute and a half.

It's only thoughts—
your own thoughts—
that keep rewinding,
repeating, replaying,
recharging,
refiring chemicals
that keep the anger
thrashing over
and over.
Only thoughts.

Breathe in.
Out.
Let them go.

Soldier Daddy

Daddy?
Are you not listening again?
Are you still sad from the war?
The army took you away,
my laughing Daddy,
turned you into a soldier.
You fought for peace.
Everyone says
I should be proud.
I am proud.
But mostly,
I want my laughing
Daddy back.

Dominoes

On this earth
we are
connected
one to
another
to another
to another
to another
to another
to another
to another
to another
to another
to another
to another
to another
to another
to another
to another
such that
whatever
happens to
one of us
happens
to
all
of

us.

No In-Between

If one is right
the other wrong
how can we ever
get along?

Tough Act

Where
there
is
fear
peace
walks a
tightrope.

Big Shoes

Peace needs big shoes,
a wide stance,
tall and resolute;
and even then
can be blown away

with

one

incautious

word.

Water and Stone

The stone stands,
solid and unmoving.
The water flows,
soft and fluid,
etching its mark
bit by infinitesimal bit.
Which is stronger?

Both.

From a Story in the Paper

The hamster was
meant to be lunch.
Put in the cage to be
eaten by a snake,
swallowed
down whole
and later digested.
But maybe the snake
was more lonely
than hungry;
perhaps he simply
hesitated
one moment
too long,
catching a look
in his lunch's
eyes,
and could not
be the cause
of the hamster's
demise.
In any case
for whatever reason
the snake neglected
to eat his lunch
and now
has a cage-mate,
friendship accepted.

One Moment

In the midst of shouting
voices, honking
horns, ringing
phones, blaring
music and the incessant
chatter of the television,
take one moment . . .
one small moment . . .
and listen
to the stillness
within
and
beneath
it all.

CRASH BAM!

BEEP! Hey!

Bla bla bla

Ringggg HONK!

No!

When...

I treat you
as I want you
to treat me
even when
you are upset
even when
I am upset
then
we
can have
peace.

Truce

Deer,
poised to munch
my geraniums.
Me,
peering at you
through the window.
We stand,
you and I,
in suspended animation.
I could **shout!**
and send you leaping,
left to eat
the scrawny weeds
or . . .
I could back away
and let you feast
on my well-tended
flowers.

Peace Is

when all
of *them*
are us.

What If?

What if angry words
vanished like
soap bubbles
and punches landed light
as butterfly kisses?
What if guns
fired marshmallow bullets,
and bombs burst
into feather clouds
sending us into fits
of giggles?
What if
we all died
laughing?

Peace Sign

Peace
When you say the word
peace peace peace
even without thinking
peace
what it means
peace peace peace
it shapes your mouth
peace peace peace peace peace
into a smile.
Peace

Pass It On

Peace. Pass it on. Peace. Pass it on. Peace. Pass it on. Peace. Pass it on. Peace. Pass it on. Peace. Pass it on. Peace.

How?

Can peace
creep up on us,
seep into our souls,
or do we have to
search it out,
coax it,
give it space?
Can you have
a piece of peace?
Can you sip it?
Can it sleep
to awaken . . .
. . . how?
Does it answer
to a whisper
or a shout?
Or how about
a prayer?

THE PEACEMAKERS

Mohandas Gandhi (1869–1948)

"Be the change you want to see in the world."

Mohandas Gandhi used passive resistance in his life-long struggle for human equality, dignity, freedom from exploitation, injustice, and violence in South Africa, India, and Pakistan. He often fasted to show the need for nonviolence. When he was seventy-eight years old, Gandhi was killed by an assassin. The Indian people gave him the name Mahatma, meaning Great Soul.

Dorothy Day (1897–1980)

"People say, 'What is the sense of our small effort?' They cannot see that we must lay one brick at a time, take one step at a time."

Dorothy Day was an American Catholic who, troubled by the poverty and unfair labor practices in the 1930s, founded the *Catholic Worker*, a newspaper that called on its readers to act upon social injustices. As a result, thirty-three homes for those in need were set up across the country.

Mother Teresa (1910–1997)

"We can do no great things, only small things with great love."

At the age of twelve, an Albanian girl named Agnes Gonxha Bojaxhiu felt a calling to serve God. She became a nun, taking the name Sister Teresa, and was sent to India where she completed her vows and began working with the poor. Mother Teresa spent the rest of her life loving and caring for the poor by founding schools and the Missionaries of Charity.

Nelson Mandela (b. 1918)

"For to be free is not merely to cast off one's chains, but to live in a way that respects and enhances the freedom of others."

As a young lawyer in South Africa, Nelson Mandela joined the African National Convention and engaged in passive resistance to the National Party's apartheid policies. He spent nearly three decades in prison because of his political position, and became a symbol of the resistance movement against apartheid. After his release, Mandela was elected the first black president of South Africa.

Jimmy Carter (b. 1924)

"Unless both sides win, no agreement can be permanent."

As President of the United States, Jimmy Carter mediated the Camp David Accords (a set of peace talks between Israel and Egypt), was an advocate of environmental protection legislation, and encouraged the appointment of women and minorities to judicial positions. Carter continues to work on resolving conflict, promoting democracy, and protecting human rights.

Martin Luther King Jr. (1929–1968)

"Peace is not merely a distant goal that we seek, but a means by which we arrive at that goal."

Using nonviolent methods, Dr. King organized protests and demonstrations to gain voting rights for African Americans. In 1963, some 250,000 protesters marched on Washington, D.C., where King delivered his famous "I Have a Dream" speech. The following year, the president signed the Civil Rights Act of 1964. Four years later, Dr. King was assassinated.

Samantha Smith (1972–1985)

"Children . . . know that peace is always possible."

When Samantha Smith was ten years old, she was afraid that the United States and the Soviet Union might have a nuclear war. She wrote to President Yuri Andropov of the Soviet Union, asking him why his country wanted to "conquer the world or at least our country." He replied that his country wanted to live in peace and invited her to visit the Soviet Union. Drawing from her experiences, Samantha wrote a book, gave speeches, and made television appearances. She died in a plane crash when she was only thirteen years old.

Mattie Stepanek (1990–2004)

"We have to make peace an attitude. Then we have to make it a habit. Finally, we must decide to live peace, to share it around the world—not just talk about it."

Mattie Stepanek was born with a rare form of muscular dystrophy and knew he would not live long. When he was three, Mattie began writing poems, and when he was eleven, he made three wishes: to have his poetry published, to have Oprah Winfrey share his message of hope and peace, and to meet Jimmy Carter. All of Mattie's wishes came true, and Mattie's message continues to spread through his books, the Internet, and various organizations that keep his spirit alive.

PEACEFUL CONNECTIONS

CREATING THESE poems and quilts has been a meaningful journey, giving me an opportunity to explore ideas and ideals close to my heart. I have not been alone on this journey. While writing the poems, I was supported and encouraged by some of my writing friends. We challenged ourselves to write a poem every day, and I chose peace as a theme.

As I worked on my quilts I drew on a rich and wonderful heritage. Woven into the centuries-old tradition of quilting are the pleasure of creating beautiful and useful objects, an element of storytelling, and a strong sense of community.

To quilt is to put layers of fabric together and stitch through all the layers in a decorative pattern. We usually think of quilts as colorful bedcovers. In the early twentieth century and before, women often used scraps left over from making clothing, or even the still usable bits of fabric from worn-out shirts and dresses, which they carefully cut and sewed together in patchwork patterns to use as the tops for their quilts. The patterns they used, often shared with one another, had names drawn from their everyday lives—Maple Leaf, Churn Dash, Log Cabin, Bear's Paw, Friendship Star. Their quilting gave them an opportunity to create and tell their stories.

When the women had tops ready to quilt, they would gather at a quilting bee. Quilting bees were times for sharing food, news, and friendship as the women worked together to make beautiful warm bedcovers from scraps that might otherwise have been thrown away.

Today, quilts are not just for beds. Many are made as wall hangings, clothing, sculpture, even bowls and baskets. Modern quilters still stitch together layers of fabric, but may often incorporate paints, printing techniques, or other materials such as paper, foils, or wood for texture and shape. The creators of these works are art quilters, expressing their

ideas and feelings in quilts. A few, like me, use various quilting techniques as illustrations for books.

One thing that has not changed is that quilters still get together. All around the world women—and now some men—gather in quilt guilds to share their love of creating quilts. I belong to the Pacific Piecemakers Quilt Guild, which has about 110 members. In addition to the monthly guild meetings, some of us get together in small groups where more experienced quilters help beginners, and we bounce ideas off one another or show off our latest project. The guild also meets to make quilts for people who are sick or bereaved and for wounded soldiers.

When I was working on this book and knew I wanted to add words on two of the quilts, I experimented with stencils and stamps, but wasn't happy with the results. I asked one of my friends, who often stamped words onto her quilts, for advice. She suggested I try silk-screening. "Talk to Judy," she said. "She has a Thermo fax machine that can make a screen for you." Judy was more than happy to make the screens, but didn't have any silk left. Another friend offered to share her silk, but then I needed a frame. I sent an e-mail to the group and two members immediately offered to loan frames. Times and methods have changed, the looks of the quilts have changed, but the sense of community, the storytelling, and sharing the joy of creating something beautiful or useful have not.

Most of the time I spend writing or quilting, I am by myself. But I am not alone. My fellow writers and quilters are with me, all of those who will one day read my words and see my pictures are with me, and even those who

won't are with me. All of us together in one world. The trick is to be mindful of that connection.

For all peacemakers, especially the young ones
—A. G. H.

Henry Holt and Company, LLC
Publishers since 1866
175 Fifth Avenue
New York, New York 10010
mackids.com

Library of Congress Cataloging-in-Publication Data
Peaceful pieces : poems and quilts about peace / by Anna Grossnickle Hines. — 1st ed.
p.   cm.
ISBN 978-0-8050-8996-7
1. Peace—Juvenile poetry. I. Title.
PS3558.I528P43 2011
811'.54—dc22
2010011697

First Edition—2011
The handmade quilts used as illustrations in this book were reproduced in full color.
The original quilts are the same size as printed.

Printed in December 2010 in China by Imago, Shenzhen, Guangdong Province, on acid-free paper. ∞

1 3 5 7 9 10 8 6 4 2